ELEANOR SMALL

# The Wish Fish

with interactive CD-ROM

## Retold by Lesley Sims

## Illustrated by Mike Gordon

Reading Consultant: Alison Kelly
Roehampton University

This story is about

Bob,  Bet,

the sea,

big fish,

small
fish

and a
magic fish.

3

Bob and Bet live
by the sea.

They like fish.

# Bob fishes all day.

He catches
big fish...

...and small fish.

# One day, he catches...

# ...a magic fish!

The fish gives Bob and
Bet three wishes.

15

"I wish to be rich," says Bob.

"I wish to be richer," says Bet.

19

"I wish to be richer still!" she says.

"Too greedy!"
says the fish.

# PUZZLES

## Which order should the pictures be in?

## Puzzle 1

A

B

C

D

## Puzzle 2

A

B

C

D

# Puzzle 3

A

B

C

D

# Puzzle 4

A

B

C

D

# Puzzle 5

Match the words to the picture.

Bet     boots     bird     bones

broom    bowl    Bob

# Puzzle 6

## What does Bob wish for?

# What does Bet wish for?

What would
you wish for?

29

# Answers to puzzles

## Puzzles 1-4

ADCB

BCAD

DBCA

ACDB

## Puzzle 5

Bob    bones    Bet

bird

bowl

boots    broom

Bob wished for

Bet wished for

# About The Wish Fish

The Wish Fish is based on an old folk tale. It is popular in many countries, from Germany to India. The story was probably first told in Russia, where it is known as The Golden Fish.

Digital illustration by Carl Gordon
Designed by Louise Flutter

This edition first published in 2009 by Usborne Publishing Ltd.,
Usborne House, 83-85 Saffron Hill, London EC1N 8RT, England.
www.usborne.com
Copyright © 2009, 2007 Usborne Publishing Ltd.